More Praise for *Album of Not*

Eve Linn's first collection glows with the feminine. Here are poems that navigate the female body and experience in unexpected language, imagery, and form. Though the title poem urges the reader to "excise the image" it's impossible. Unforgettable images reverberate throughout every poem bringing astonishment. Linn's craft forces our lyric understanding in the layers of meaning she brings to her reader's attention. The narrative unfolds in the voice of mother, daughter, bride, witness as well as the personas of Frida Kahlo, Sarah Bernhardt, and Francesca Woodman. This is a book to return to again and again. To paraphrase Linn – *you will sip with your eyes*. Read these poems with your heart.
— **Anastasia Vassos**, author of *NOSTOS*

Album of Not's speaker admits to being "spread empty," and calls herself "a case of mistaken," yet learns to "prefer her own imperfect relics." A palpable immediacy permeates the search for history and self: "Nothing is too small to shine," including memories of the "green of bud break / spathes of skunk cabbage / moss velvet of my best dress." There's no way not to admire both her pluck and the vital throb of her language: "Tired of wait, I kissed myself alive." Yes!

— **Ellen Doré Watson**, author of *pray me stat eager*

ALBUM OF NOT

EVE F. W. LINN

Nixes Mate Books
Allston, Massachusetts

Copyright © 2024 Eve F. W. Linn

Book design by d'Entremont
Cover photograph used with permission.

All rights reserved. This book or any portion thereof may not be reproduced or used in any manner whatsoever without the express written permission of the publisher except for the use of brief quotations in a book review or scholarly journal.

Library of Congress Control Number: 2024932024

ISBN 978-1-949279-54-2

Nixes Mate Books
POBox 1179
Allston, MA 02134
nixesmate.pub

"We look at the world once, in childhood. The rest is memory."
— Louise Glück

CONTENTS

I

I Hang My Dress from a Hole in the Sky	3
Mare	4
When I was Pregnant and Sucked Lemons	5
Accident on a corner in Mexico City, 1925	6
Amniocentesis	7
Mourning Picture, 1890	8
Period	9
Impossible Blue	10
On the Verge	12
Henry Ford Hospital, 1932	13
After Hip Surgery	15
Frau Schneider	17
Album of Not	18
Dress Up	19

II

When I Was a Door	21
Wet	27
Frida Kahlo Writes a Letter to her Monkey, Camito de Guayabal	28
My Son as Acrobat	29
Visiting Hours	30

Tatting	31
Ode to the Eye	33
Self Portrait With Thorns and Hummingbird, 1940	34
Bride	35
Night Work	36
Small Deaths	37
Empress Josephine, Dying at Malmaison, near Paris, 1814	39
Villefranche-sur-Mer, 1939	40
Just Before Rain	41

III

Bone Throb	43
Frida Kahlo Performs Open Heart Surgery on Herself	45
Wearing of the Body	46
Stieglitz Recalls An Argument, New York City, Summer 1918	47
Green	49
The Future of Apples	51
After Rain	52
San Vitale Basilica	54
Le Premier Acte	57
In The Archive	60

ALBUM OF NOT

I

"Memory – the very skin of life." — Elizabeth Hardwick

I HANG MY DRESS FROM A HOLE IN THE SKY

buttons gleam – planets in my eyes,
my dress immense –

an irregular galaxy
in this celestial sphere

words streak in eccentric orbit
awake in this stellar wind

in the attic of this night,
I am the scribe of battered stars –

MARE

All flying mane and bared teeth, she dipped and dived.
Blue rosettes at her bridle, golden tassels on her saddle
blanket. Leather reins and gilded bit. Neck arched, leaning
for the jump that never came – One more revolution,
one more turn. Her hollow body rattled. All day long,
she rose and fell. All day long, her sides kicked by small
feet, her bit yanked by sticky hands, sweet with sweat.
My mother circled, saying nothing.

WHEN I WAS PREGNANT AND SUCKED LEMONS

I knew you would be a boy. Dreams bucked
my nights. My belly grew – a round hardness,
gleamed. I should have known strange things would
follow. Wild dreams, fatigue, nausea. I needed no food.

I wanted to ride with you between waves.
With foam on my flanks, seaweed on my shoulders,
we dove and surfaced. Our skins sparkled with salt.
Wet as you were after birth before wildness went.

ACCIDENT ON A CORNER IN MEXICO CITY, 1925

after Frida Kahlo

A handrail crossed my womb. Perforated my vagina.
My pelvis, an inhospitable sieve. Ferrous
pool, sacred wolves sup at crusted edges.
What is the weight of blood, of bone, of breath –
God did not take me then.

Pierced, pierced not by arrows.
Seamed with a curved carpet needle and catgut.
My body, braille of stitches, achitecture of fragments.
Ossuary.

My hands unbroken. My eyes clear. So clear.
Mis manos estan intactas, mis ojos son claros, tan claros.
A skeleton wired with fireworks slept above me.
Un regalo, una bendición.

Bound with plaster and leather. Blazoned
with satin-stitched flowers the size of planets – resplendent
as my mother's ancestors *antepassados de la madre*
grit of sugar skulls crunched sweet between my teeth,
I am my own.

AMNIOCENTESIS

I dreamed girl dreams. My love for you
slow to come. At sixteen weeks, my jelled belly
bared to needle. I wiggled my toes turned
away from the doctor's hand. Sliver of hollow
silver pushed in, sucked out pale baby piss.
The sonogram showed shadows, an out of focus
weather map. Your pulsing heart amplified,
one hundred and sixty beats a minute. First
picture, blurred map of boy.

MOURNING PICTURE, 1890

after Edwin Romanzo Elmer

Mother is small, black-bonneted, upright
in the rocking chair. Her glance criss-crosses Father's.
Bowler-hatted, knees bent, he holds a newspaper
or a handkerchief. A cat, spotted, tail vertical, stops mid-step.
I am larger than my parents. I collar my pet lamb.
A lace fichu crescents my shoulders.

Behind me, our house proud on granite blocks,
tilts, I think. Corbels strain to hold the roof.
My hair, braided, bound for sleep. My china doll,
brought from faraway, fills the wicker carriage.
My black straw hat sashed with red streamers.
They will not rise without wind.
Lucy, my doll, will always stay the same size.

PERIOD

After the slap all good jewish girls get
(and of course all jewish girls are good),
after the warnings all good jewish
girls get about pre-marital sex (and all jewish
girls are good after the warnings, especially
from their mothers and grandmothers,
may their memories be a blessing,
even if they are really pushy know-it-alls
who just happen to look in your underwear
drawer or in your medicine cabinet once
they know you are a woman or maybe
they are just trying to remember one
sweet stolen kiss before the world ignited
when there were only dead jews), after that slap
rouged my cheek with the imprint of my mother's
fingers, every month, as I shed my own flesh,
my eggs, smaller than fish roe, found the sea.

IMPOSSIBLE BLUE

Light, the color of light, that's what I remember.
        The light after a hot, cloudless day
when my skin smelled of chlorine and *Coppertone*

fingers sticky with melted ice cream from a Good
        Humor pop. The smooth pale stick from
Baltic birch, plunged into sweet vanilla melt

studded with crunch, I swept my tongue around
        my teeth to get it all, all that I could
scavenge, leave nothing over. Later I would

swallow his bitter gift almost choking, proud
        I could, without vomiting. That hot
gush of someone's future need.

I washed the easy afternoon away, stopping
        to admire thin strips of white
skin left by bathing suit straps, my shoulder

sunburnt, stinging, just visible in the steam
        fogged mirror above the porcelain
sink, scents of a body inching toward fullness,

furred crotch, armpits, vanished by *Summer's Eve* and *Secret*
       I wanted to stay in the tub, water cooling, one leg
just over the rim, my foot touching terry cloth,

my arm reaching for a towel, my baby
       doll pajamas ironed smooth, the slap of rubber
flip-flops on the bare stairs. Dinner on the porch.

Now in the future that is the present, I remembered
       I remember not shame, not exactly, but a
question, kept folded away –

Out that far beyond the deep end of the pool, where
       the lifeguard would blow his whistle if he
thought you couldn't swim.

ON THE VERGE

In the electric air, perched on the hard ledge
of the bathtub, I smelled pine needles, burning dust.

Inscrutable as a Sybil, submerged in still water,
your body. One arm dangling over the rim.

Your breasts – rust brown circles surround elongated
 nipples. Sunflowers, I thought. Mine, a small rise, nub pink.

I curled my toes on the bathmat. You stood up.
Along the bottom of the tub, your heels squelched.

You bent to pull the stopper, buttocks puckered,
your spine a string of buttons with no dress –

Folded over yourself – a small wingless bird,
with no feathers for cover. A tangle, your pubic hair.

A spiral of honey bees rises from a domed glass bottle.

HENRY FORD HOSPITAL, 1932

after Frida Kahlo

Sky cyanotic. Clouds cough. Grass dark as an anvil. Far behind me the world of men stretches to the horizon. Smokestacks and water towers, buildings stacked one on top of another. A ribbon links city to city. The relentless conveyor belt of parts swings over men's heads. Blast furnaces roar hot tongues, flames stagger towards distant stars. *Feed me, Feed me more.* Insatiable beast. I shout to make myself heard. Whistles shriek. No one can hear me. I cannot hear anyone. Flowers bloom and shrivel in an instant, incinerated. I am always in between.

Bed linen gorged with my blood. Tissues of the unborn, the baby I can never hold. Folded, blunt headed, feet crossed at the ankles, arms gesture a prayer – protesting his expulsion. I hold him anyway – thin red threads from navel to navel – he floats above me, above the bed, the bed that should have held us both. I am spread empty. Belly domed, knees a bridge – a passage where sharps cut and tore. Pubic hair a dark nest, a sliver against pale flesh.

Twisted – a batt of gauze to staunch. Clots, tissue, viscera. You – covered in transparent film veins blue. No breath from the branches of your lungs, no cry. Smaller than a plucked chicken at a market stall. I fought to hold you, keep you close until I could do the only thing to save you. Paint you, still nameless, but holy. Cohesion of our cells.

What ties me to this earth – Betrayed by my own body. Slow crawl as the stillborn child culled from my labyrinth. (*pain, o so familiar, the slow burn, the ravish of a lover.*) Each scar opened again, again. It must be this way. Sutures hum inside me. Labia fringed as orchid petals. I wanted only to paint my child, but no. Robber gloved hands took you away, fed you to steel jaws shining under a hanging bulb.

What are the works of men – I prefer my own imperfect relics. I will return in the arms of the moon.

AFTER HIP SURGERY

You tilt your cheek
the chamois creases

of your face towards me
the universal sign for *kiss me,*

In that picture, that one, lost
you were the *White Rock Girl*

icon of carefree stenciled
on deep green glass bottles.

I don't want any water, will people
stop asking me if I want water —

without footrests your feet dangle
long yellowed nails catch on

cashmere socks I worry over your
knobbed toes, up toward

your instep up to your ankle
while you stare down the hallway.

Your body so small – no edges
touch the sheepskin seat
your thin hair, a spider's thread.

FRAU SCHNEIDER

Her gutturals, mustache, hag jaw
tinctures and foul teas filled the apartment.
Only my mother approved:
Her references are impeccable.

My silent father didn't interfere except once.
On Christmas Eve she stewed rabbit. The swinging door
wrenched open, my father burst into the kitchen,
What is that God Damned awful smell? Thick as a spell.
I didn't know people ate rabbits –

I knew the caged one in the science room at school.
Silent except for a tiny sucking sound at its water spout.
Now, a furless animal, its mottled skin, sizzling in fat.

Still she stayed in the room behind the kitchen.
No one guessed the cause of my nightmares and tantrums.
No one asked. In the dark the rabbit grew long teeth.

Lights snapped on. Her tight daytime screw of hair
braided in a grey tail, angry red flushed her cheeks.
Her nightgown ballooned. She hissed spit.

Lights snapped off.
I waited for the rabbit to eat me.

ALBUM OF NOT

The object is to excise the image until the knife falls.
Keep going. Pile up these cut-outs. One on top of another.
Do it again. Do it. Press hard so the edges do not fray.
Excise the image.
Leave only a perfect silhouette. A perfect emptiness.
Press down against the glossy paper. Press hard.
Use a very sharp knife. The object is to excise the image.
Do it.

DRESS UP

Swathed in Nana's mink stole,
boxy purse across my wrist
nugget of clasp snapped
sharp. My head turban
twisted. A shiny compact
round, filled with pink powder.
Mirror the size of a blink.
Parts of my face. Half an eye,
nostril, lips, milk teeth. High
heels drown my feet, stumble
for balance. Still, I strike a pose.
Smile, tilt a hip, a see-saw stuck
on up. I wait for what I want
in make believe. Or not. *Oh, she's
a regular little Sarah Bernhardt!*
I didn't know who Sarah was, but
thought she must be happy.

II

"You cannot see me from where I look at myself."
— Francesca Woodman

WHEN I WAS A DOOR

after Francesca Woodman

I am door, I am frame, I am jamb, I am lintel,

    I am threshold, am hinge, am pivot, am screw.

I am   a jar,   I am closed, I am key h o l e.

I am close t, I am hang er, I am hook, I am handle,

    I am edge, I am corner, I am crevice.

        windowpaneglass.

I am b r o ken, I am s hard, I am s p l i n t e r, I am s liver,

    am scrape am scab am slice am scar.

I am bite, I am teeth, I am tongue, I am lips.

swayswivelswerveskid.

am swan, am goose girl, am story, am tale, am fable

am feral, am pleasure, am purr

I am eye/ I am retina/ I am iris/I am sclera/ I am sight/

I am shutter/I am pupil/I am eyelid/ I am lens/ I am peep/

I am gaze I am gazer

glimpse,   GLANCE

GLARE

                        a
   s

                            k
                                a
                        n
                                c
              e

I am confound, am caprice, am disdain, am disquiet,
am   d
     i
        s   a   r
    r
         a
         y

~~TROUBLE~~

   tangle   tear

TORMENT

teeththroattongue

torrent

tempest

I am torque,   I am t
                      o
           r   n   I am
          I am twist   t
                               u
                                m
                               u
                       l
                               t
   I am skin,   am scorch,

              I am singe,
                         am sear,
I am sinister,

              am single

am body/ am spine/am vertebrae/am pelvis /am pubis /am bone

I am imposter, I am fool I am folly, I am fail,

f
a
l
l
e
n

I am feign I am feint I am fay am furtive am foreign

am flung I am far I am fair

I am fester, I am decay, I am spoil, I am blot,

I am crumble, I am molder,

I am light, I am flare, I am blaze, I am burn,

am shadow,

am fade,

am hide,

am not

I am gust

I am feather I am wing I am flight

    am   d
     i

        s
s   o

          l
           v
                e

WET

After eighteen hours of labor, you inched down
toward day. Me, a hinge of protest. No mind, but
expulsion. Contractions and caesuras until the bed
fell away. At once, your head parted my legs, burned
out of me. Before blood and womb juices wiped away.
Before naked frog limbs, skin creases, nail seeds,
coiled ears. Your lips curved with pink lust,
rooted for satisfaction. Garments too harsh
to dress your newness.

FRIDA KAHLO WRITES A LETTER TO HER MONKEY, CAMITO DE GUAYABAL

after several self-portraits

dear only offspring of my body,
a body no longer whole or
fruitful, scraped to shards,
hinged, nailed with hidden
spikes, corseted to itself,
skin picked out in sutures,

lustful joker – in your eyes
deep forest grief – your once
home, before abduction by a man
with a truck full of cages – you barked
all torqued pain –

once you ate ripe fruits, caught
despite your wiles, now you twine
coarse furred arms, hook black
hands around my neck.

MY SON AS ACROBAT

My little somersault, I did not know
darkness touched you, when
you rolled out of me, puckered.

You chose silence, kept secrets.
Held up by urchins on a rough
plank, you balanced between worlds.

Lived on the heady perfume of linden
blossoms beloved by bees. Your motley
diamonds of blue and yellow.

I sewed without cease, unable to fix
tears. Your face, wide and open,
a soup spoon. I could sip from your eyes.

VISITING HOURS

Between the hours of three and five, a uniform behind glass
decides if I can be your mother.

This floor gives nothing. These cold corridors. This hard school.
Never say what you think. Practice jargon. Erase yourself.

My life searched. No sharp objects allowed. No strings. No food.
Metal door opens from the inside. Sheer want in your stare.

Bent to hug, each vertebrae hard against my arms.
Your lips chapped, your breath hot, your eyes naked.

A half-man half-woman in gypsy earrings says, *Sit here.*
We hold hands on the plastic cushioned sofa.

Visiting hours are over in five minutes. You stand. I memorize you.
Your gray suede sneakers flop with no laces.

TATTING

19th century handwork for making especially durable lace from a series of knots and loops.

Unravel gown, unpick stitches with my teeth
trouble for a needle, sharpen a splinter with glass
until it's a glossy beak singing

Thread thimble tamp down
       as in extinguish
              as in fire
                      as in stifle

Scarce company – I whisper in between my ears – hair gone
a nest they said for lice – before my mirror I sat with the
monogramed silver brush and huddle of hairpins
counting – the loose strands saved for a switch

Tassel trinket tight
       as in corset
              as in constrain
                      as in contain

Castile soap and chamomile in the rinse water.
A summer's day – a calendar ago I charted currents,
noted shoals, buoys, sand bars, light houses

I waded – my bare toes schools of fish, wind
leaves letters I must learn.
Sailboats tack – race circling terns

My fingers urgent to thread, to knit – to count
each loop as my dearest – to knit each new
held in my arms their bodies blind me with bright writhe

Here a cold bedstead, here the thin ticking, here the bucket
the door swings

Tit thigh tongue
       as in bitten
              as in silent
                     as in wither.

ODE TO THE EYE

Honey harvested in King Solomon's time
        rows of terra cotta jars
in the desert of Tel Rehov,
        city of bees
hives slick with propolis
        honest home of the queen

wolf tree in an open field furrowed in green
        light spreads to the roof peak
the glass eyes of the cupola
        on the barn – windows burn gold
but there is no fire

fat green buds of peonies
        threaded with ants
so heavy they shatter after rain
        litter of petals – upturned
silent – blushed and wet.

SELF PORTRAIT WITH THORNS AND HUMMINGBIRD, 1940

after Frida Kahlo

Mi hijo's fingers plait thorns
I wear as a necklace, absorbed
with his intricate play, head cocked
nostrils flared by blood's ferrous
urge, weaving me a cape,
not just a necklace or a crown.
White butterflies find a home
in my hair.

And the pendant, a hummingbird
its over-fluttering heartbeat
batter of wings, now cold,
nestled at the pulse in my throat,
while the cat glares. His swiftness
missed this meal. No supple bones,
no scanty meat.

BRIDE

after Francesca Woodman

I turn my body into the white skin of birches,
wrap my identities into the same face.
I am a case of mistaken.

Sometimes, there are four of me.
Hide and seek. Dress and undress.
I look under everything.

Hands sooty as swallows, nails close-bitten.
Only my body in a chair.
By my feet, stain spreads. My shadow.

NIGHT WORK

I hear you before you are awake. Settle your blanketed
weight across my lap. You mewl louder, root, twist.
Toes arch, grip with each suck, swallow. At 2 a.m.,
another hunger speaks – an owl's call joins yours.

Hour of mothers and children, one feeds the other. No –
both feed. As lips nuzzle nipple, sweet milk showers.
No thought of more than pull and pulse.

More important than sleep, I make your present.
Made and undone each minute. More important than sleep,
I listen through cracks on night's edge.

SMALL DEATHS

Two nights in a row, a field mouse
overcome – a small scuffle of air,
not even loose papers move,
but the mouse, almost invisible
on the oriental rug, figured
with the patterns of paradise
stops breathing.

There is no puncture or dark blood,
its naked legs and transparent
toes curled like eyelashes
do not move, the tail hangs limp.
I am the undertaker. I offer
the body wrapped in several sheets
of *Bounty*.

Dusk – I almost step on a moth.
I hold the edge of one copper
wing, startled at the agitation
between my fingers, its body rigid,
but wings, because they are wings
must move, urge upward.

Between door and crack of air,
I toss this flyer out to catch a draft.
Later, drawn off-course by artificial light,
they will cluster close around the porch
bulb – a haze of gauze –

EMPRESS JOSEPHINE, DYING AT MALMAISON, NEAR PARIS, 1814

Privy to loose tongues and eager thighs, I learn silence.
A sigh, a nod, the narrowing of an eye, an effective snare.
A snap of a fan, a warm pulse below my throat, a gown only of thread.

Damasks, centifloras, bourbons, gallicas, china teas,
noisettes. I stroke your petals, inhale your scent.

Black swans, mated for life, swim in endless circles
round a lake of artifice. No heir. I am cast away.

I dream. Fevered voice, *Beware the thorns.*
In my room of red and gold, I think only of our long nights.
The ceiling, a cloud puffed sky.

But, most of all roses. This richness – this intoxicated heat.
Cinnamon, clove, cognac and musk perfumes everything.

VILLEFRANCHE-SUR-MER, 1939

after an unknown photographer

Who took that photograph of me
beyond the wall lashed with flames –
Below, the deep harbor, flat and blue as a plate
I cannot see it –
Sleeves rolled to the elbow, I am writing a letter.
No, I am painting. Engulfed by wildflowers.

Is it mid-day –
My eyes squint against the glare,
against the ferris wheel face of sunflowers.

I burn white. Folds of my skirt flicker –
Poplars brush a corner of the sky.
I turn, annoyed at the interruption. I cannot stop.
It is just my life, *wild and eccentric*, spooling
unspooling, on sheet after sheet.

Note: Villefranche-sur-Mer was the hiding place of the German-Jewish artist, Charlotte Salomon (1917-1943).

JUST BEFORE RAIN

Who has not wanted to be cloud
at least once
to leave the body – bones
in silent disruption one
molecule at a time, so easy
unlike death that costs a coffin,
if not more – much more –
undertakers, those crows that guide
varnished coffins under
ground to the kingdom of smalls –
those miners of decay –
those earth turners

III

"It is not enough to photograph the obviously picturesque."
— Dorothea Lange

BONE THROB

after Francesca Woodman

Tired of the wait, I kissed myself live.
    Breast against thigh. Dip of clavicle,
tender as a puddle. Nose to knee crouched.
    I have swum long in sleep.
I eavesdrop on earth worms,
    I dig in their tunnels, my fingers limned
with casings, their shed skins.
    This – my kingdom of under.
I know where vixens and kits gamble.
    I know green secrets of summoning.
Such sounds, chir, thrum, scrape then nothing,
    not silence, there is never silence
when you cup hands to lap water
    when wet lips touch&part, when bones throb
when a storm is close.
    What charms do I carry –
The wrist I broke at twelve, the cuts
    healed now. Blood and flesh,
water pinking, drain a blank eye.
    I watched myself until I couldn't, until
spill of limbs felled me.
    I traced hexagons, black tiles white grout.
Bees circled, wrapped my body in hum.

I promised you a message. Look up.
Look up at the sky. Watch clouds.
　　　There is my body and yours.
You know I was here –
　　　dragged heel marks in the tall grass, pearl button,
strip of photos from a fun fair, stub of lipstick.
　　　Not all angels have wings.

FRIDA KAHLO PERFORMS OPEN HEART SURGERY ON HERSELF

after Frida Kahlo

Sever myself from what I love most – I open
my chest, peel back my breast and reach in

to the pouch of pulses, excise his small head,
pass it to my other whose hand I hold

then poppies burst, bleed, stain,
that white skirt that curtains this broken

body, inescapable – the body I inhabit
my body contains continents, the new world and the old
world that mingle in my blood, a globe, a centrifuge.

WEARING OF THE BODY

Light glories in a derelict warehouse. Nothing can contain it. Windows show only shine. Each day I begin. Unroll the rough cloth. I practice cutting. A lily grows in my hands.
>What bounty – imperfection – veins in shrivel, leaf in curl
>What of sigh and breath of cleaved rock
>What of blade and maul

All I want is to feel the weight of feather upon feather on my shoulders. *This is the message. Grow wings.* I have no choice.

With each feather, I gasp. This growing pain. My scapula pricked, then pierced. Wild stunned. *Bare it.*
>I kneel on dirty cement, breathless
>What of this sleeve of skin,
>its bones, what holds together –
>What exists beneath
>>shear   sunder   splinter

And that dip beneath the throat, where words gather and mingle, where pulse is visible,
rising and falling, where the smell of oranges hovers.
>What of blood – both red & blue by alchemy of oxygen
>Savor on the tongue, (iron, rust, metal & flake)
>>flow   clot   staunch

>that monthly wedding with the moon

STIEGLITZ RECALLS AN ARGUMENT, NEW YORK CITY, SUMMER 1918

after Alfred Stieglitz

I'm sure it was Japanese,
that kimono, a peace offering

after an argument, just crossed over
your breasts like wings or maybe

just the pattern of flying cranes
said to be auspicious.

As you lounged, you odalisque,
I remember the pale oval

of your face brushed with brows
your unbound hair

trailed down your arms –
those wild mustangs of your girlhood

your clavicles, your neck urgent
taut with muscles

you did not want me
so I sat in the straight chair

watched steel going up
beam upon beam girder to girder

your hands almost serene

GREEN

I can't remember words. The nurse, bent over my bed,
fingers flat on my wrist, counting.

But that day – that day – dirt between my winter white toes
back from the woods and stream, green of bud break,

glacial crawl – leavings – ice scoured fragments –
this ground – this slurry of time

here, a swell, here a run of sap, here, a smell of sweet damp
those young years breathed green – stone walls beckoned.

I balance, precarious, one foot in front of the other,
my hair blows behind me, then in my eyes,

I squint into the sun, tip my head back on purpose
to see through the scrim of leaves, dizzy pieces of sky and clouds

whisked like egg whites in grandmother's beehive bowl from Ohio
toes curled inside my wet Keds.

Spathes of skunk cabbage, peepers pitched call at dusk.
Father's prized cats-eye marble, mother's heirloom emerald.

Moss velvet of my best dress, and how louvered shutters made slices of sun on the pine floor each morning.

I raise my arms, my hands hold the air, a wreath of all my years. Bent over the bed, she feels for my carotid pulse.

THE FUTURE OF APPLES

Remove spurs that do not fruit,
dry wood, water sprouts or green
wood that crosses another branch.
One rubs another, bruises bark,
causes cankers, then rots.

In gloved hand, curved
shears wait, oiled and ready.
Dive close. Cut slant and quick.
Sever the twig, still
sap-filled, clear, juicy-sweet.

A clean cut with a sharp blade
is always best. Expose the wound.
To sun, to dry, to harden, to callus.
The burn pile is full of twigs
cut for good reason.

AFTER RAIN

Sky scoured. Wisps of cloud cover that impossible blue without a name. That blue of molten cobalt when blown through a pipe created my grandmother's angel, from Murano.

That island of glass blowers, a vaporetto ride from Venice – over that history of water.

The guide's loud voice, in heavily accented English warns of departure time. He is eager for a shot of grappa and a cigarette in his neighborhood cafe.

Tourists scurry on narrow footpaths, crowd the doors of pastel painted houses.

The smooth blankness that betrays nothing of the making, the shadowed folds of her robe, hem upturned, knees bent, her naked heels a penance.

From her lips silent devotions trace cartwheels – the clouds of fork-tailed tree swallows returning every spring.

Birch leaves lucent green, haired to the touch, their catkins dangle like small scrolls, holy as a mezuzah once fixed to the door frames of the faithful.

What is left – Ghost prints and screw holes. Tossed in the streets after a raid, the paper turning to wet pulp streaming black ink.

Soil so avid for rain there are no puddles. Grass satisfied settles in shadow. Clenched cerise buds of the crab apples open white – bees plummet to their center mad with hunger to fulfill their ordained role in the hive.

Beneath this tree, planted almost thirty years ago, the blossoms shaken by rain drop to the ground in a shuffle. Each the size of a child's finger tip.

And now there is a long stretch of clouds weaving in and out among the leaves fuller than before –

Does white (the color that is all colors) make blue bluer – Backlit clouds curl to white fire. Nothing too small to shine.

SAN VITALE BASILICA

built in Ravenna ca. 6Th century, to honor the martyrdom of Saint Vitalis, a Roman slave

Suffered the rack   what is known about the Saint
buried alive for his faith

    here under my feet

On the Adriatic Coast   what is known of the location
licked by salt and swamps

    eighty miles south of Venice

by imperial decree, a basilica

Built of *terra cotta* bricks   what is known about the construction
each singular, each the color of skin

    pressed in rough molds

Four angels support the vault
wings alert   what is seen inside the basilica

    poised to fly

Glass, gold dug from dross, then
polished by hand
                                                            what stories are on the walls
      fruit trees and vines

A hallelujah of prophets
Evangelists, their mascots

      angel, lion, ox and eagle

Isaac bound on a rock
Abraham's hand ready

      instead a fine fat ram dies

I am indifferent to miracles   my dilemma
those show stoppers

      Why should God bend over

backwards to do me any favors?

Doves seek night
heads tucked near sleep

      cafe tables cast shadows

not quite halos

A cat slinks – hunts   what is holy
fat vermin or tourist trash

    a saint's card rolls in dust

Squares of tesserae once   what is known of art
molten in a furnace

    backed by gold and silver leaf

Each hand-cut tile irregular
glints and glows as flesh

    then the master counts out squares to arch a brow

LE PREMIER ACTE

I adored my mother, but with a touching and fervent desire to leave her, never to see her again, to sacrifice her to God. – Sarah Bernhardt, My Double Life

With a mewl, wet dragged with blood, I left the womb. As all of us, yes, even those rich men who paid for pleasure. They had no cause to recall this moment. These men could decide my future. My birth an inconvenience for Maman.

Early years spent far from Paris on the rocky coast of Brittany. My convent education cursory. I was ornament. Unwilling. Ungovernable. Fits overcame me. Mother Superior alone could soothe me.

I acted for the first time at a fête for the visiting Monsignor. I had learned all the lines for the leading role. Did I divine my future then – still a child of not yet fifteen. I only knew that I must decide for myself.

Maman, advised by a wealthy habitué, decided I would audition for the Conservatoire. The acting school for the Comédie Française. That evening I saw my first performance. As the great velvet curtain rose, as the great chandeliers dimmed, I had no doubts. Acting would be my life.

I possessed a strong instinct for understanding what passed between a woman and a man. My childhood governed by these small gestures, the tilt of a head, the pressure of a hand, that always gave away the truth.

The smile that was not a smile –
As I walked the streets of Paris, I silently recited my audition piece. I noticed the cut and drape of that season's gown, the pale ankle, next to the dark boot, the scent of baking bread, flowers tall in tin buckets, stems tied with twine, swathed in paper. Already skilled at observation – the drama of the smallest exchange. I needed only practice and knowledge of the classics. The great authors and their words. I would bring them to life as no one before me.

No one could make up their minds about me. Was I beautiful, was I talented, did I have a future – So young, I stood before the examiners and recited one of La Fontaine's fables, Les Deux Pigeons, captivating them with my voice, my eyes that changed color with the light. Still ungovernable, my restless temper made me resign my contract due to a contretemps.

I could never fulfill my ambitions at the august Comédie, governed by tradition, noble but stultifying. My next contract at the Théâtre du Gymnase promised fine parts, and so I accepted. But it was a ruse. The fine parts became fewer and fewer. I swore to give up acting and instead bought a confectionery shop. I realized my mistake immediately.

Quel bordel. Still wishing to see me settled, Maman continued to meddle, suggesting suitors, all rejected, dismissed. Unknown to her, I had a lover of noble family, and soon was pregnant. Maman, impatient with my stubbornness, always criticized me, favoring my youngest sister. Convinced of my failures, never believing in my success. It was not one slight, but many.

At Rue Duphot, I waited for the birth of my child. I swore to be a better mother than my own. The accident of my birth did nothing to prevent my success. So I labored, staggered around the room, held on to the furniture. Pants and groans. Folded by pain. Dried sweat. Smell of salt and blood. From the bed, I saw sharp, bright instruments laid on a linen towel. *Push, Madame, and again.* The infant's high, wild cry. My lover's family not eager to claim a bastard, a title I too bore.

I would rather he not know his father at all, if my experience is worth anything. The constant longing for something you cannot have is too painful. Letters and gifts from the absent one only increase the desire for what cannot be. I will not hide the name of his father from my son, he will make his own choice to seek him out or not, when he is of age. For now, I hold my child to my breast.

IN THE ARCHIVE

So I must invent what is lost.

They're all dead now so I can't ask. I could have, years ago. I didn't. I can't ask the names of the small villages, towns, larger towns or cities. What endearments did mothers call through windows — windows overlooking the garden plot, waiting to be planted.

Whom I do most closely resemble — I can't ask.
No old photographs I can hold, scrutinize with a magnifying glass.
I can't ask why there are so few relatives.

Wind changed.

A story remembered, overheard, murmured slid underneath my door in an unknown language Was it Russian, German or Yiddish? A lullaby of syllables that sang through dreams. Somewhere is where my family lived. A place with a name that changed with the march of boots.

Two young brothers traveled overland to a port.

They live in a ledger crowded with lost names. Uniforms question. The Great Hall emptied and refilled. Coughs muffled in sleeves, pale cheeks pinched in haste, whispers to quiet children. Dry fear lodged in their mouths.

Here is the album.

Stained red velvet covers, nap worn to boards. Each corner protected with metal flourishes. The center medallion gone, its imprint dark as ripe plums. The clasp for safe keeping twisted, lost. I bought it to pretend I had a past. The photograph I am searching for is gone.

Here is the photograph.

I can see that photograph, run my fingers along its deckle edges, hold it snug in my palm. I am the girl in the black and white 3 x 5 print. I am playing dress up. My feet swim in too-large heels, my shoulders swathed in Nana's mink stole, my platinum curls topped with a hat tilted over one ear. I brandish a boxy handbag. A captive audience of parents and grandparents sits on a powder blue plastic-covered sofa.

Here I am.

Everyone said I looked like my father. I am the first grandchild.
Somehow, I knew it's important to make people happy. I struck a pose.
Laughter, rising and falling. One grandfather slapped his trousered knee.

All the heads nodded. I turned in a slow circle. *She's a regular little Sarah Bernhardt.*
I didn't know who Sarah Bernhardt was, but I knew I'd put on a great show.

ACKNOWLEDGMENTS

Poems

"Green" appeared in *Crosswinds Poetry Journal,* Volume I, 2016.

"The Future of Apples" appeared as the Poem of the Month on the *Old Frog Pond* website, February 2016.

"Wet" appeared in *The Wild Word,* the *Mother* issue, May 2017.

"On The Verge" appeared in *Cider Press Review,* Vol.19. Issue 3. October 8, 2017.

"Tatting" appeared in *Crosswinds Poetry Journal,* Spring 2020.

"Frida Kahlo Writes a Letter to her Monkey," appeared in *Lily Poetry Review,* Winter 2021.

"Villefranche-sur-Mer," appeared in *Crosswinds Poetry Journal,* Volume VI. Spring 2021.

"Ode to the Eye," appeared in *Quartet Journal,* April 2021.

"Henry Ford Hospital, 1932" appeared in *Nixes Mate Review,* Spring 2023.

"Bone Throb," appeared in *Crosswinds Poetry Journal,* Volume IX, Spring 2023.

"Stieglitz Recalls An Argument, New York City, Summer 1918," appeared in *Quartet Journal,* September 2023.

"Accident On A Corner in Mexico City, 1925" appeared in *The Power of the Feminine I: Poems from the Feminine Perspective, (The Power of the Feminine I, Volume 1)* edited by Cooper, Christal Ann Rice and Donna Biffar, (Thresh Press, January 2024)

Chapbook

Grateful acknowledgment is made to River Glass Books for publishing the following poems in the chapbook Model Home (2019): "On the Verge," originally published under the title "The Verge," "Mare," "Mourning Picture, 1890," originally published under the title "Ashfield, Massachusetts, 1890," "When I was Pregnant and Sucked Lemons," originally published under the title "When I was Pregnant," "Night Work," "Just Before Rain," originally published under the title "Kingdom of Smalls," "Wet," "I Hang My Dress from a Hole in the Sky," "Green," "The Future of Apples," and "Period".

THANK YOU

Without the support of the following individuals, this passion project would not exist.

To the incomparable July Westhale, who found the center of this collection and guided me in writing the poems that completed the manuscript.

To Joan Houlihan, long time friend and mentor who honed my writing, critical and editorial skills.

To Ellen Doré Watson and her fabulous generative workshop which helped me start writing after a long silence. To the members of this workshop who are some of the smartest and wisest people I know.

To Allison P. Davis for her loyal support and friendship.

To Amy Holman, literary consultant, who advised me on crafting book proposals.

To Sean Singer, who has expanded my knowledge of contemporary poetry through his curated newsletter and his critical reading groups.

To Ted Clausen, Lisa Kaufman and Jenny Grassl, members of my Tuesday workshop, where many of these poems got their first reading. You have enriched my life in countless ways.

To the Nixes Mate team who accepted *Album of Not* for publication. Thanks to Annie Pluto for her enthusiasm and her skillful shaping of the final manuscript. Thanks to Michael McInnis who designed a beautiful book and cover.

To my beloved family. To John, my husband who wrangles technology on my behalf and never doubted this book would find a home. To my son Evan who knows the importance of a goal. Your work ethic and determination inspire me. You changed my life by making me a mother.

To my mother Karel who surrounded me with books and encouraged my love of reading.

To my sister Kay for her enthusiastic encouragement

To my cherished feline companions, past and present.

ABOUT THE AUTHOR

Eve F. W. Linn is a poet and visual artist. She received her BA *cum laude* in Studio Art from Smith College and her MFA in Creative Writing from Lesley University. She is the author of the chapbook, *Model Home* (River Glass Books, 2019). Her poem "Bone Throb" was a finalist in the Crosswinds 2023 poetry contest. Other poems have appeared in *Adanna Literary Journal, Cider Press Review, Lily Poetry Review, Naugatuck River Review, Nixes Mate Review, Quartet Journal* and *So to Speak: Feminist Journal of Language and Art.*

42° 19' 47.9" N   70° 56' 43.9" W

Nixes Mate is a navigational hazard in Boston Harbor used during the colonial period to gibbet and hang pirates and mutineers.

Nixes Mate Books features small-batch artisanal literature, created by writers who use all 26 letters of the alphabet and then some, honing their craft the time-honored way: one line at a time.

nixesmate.pub

www.ingramcontent.com/pod-product-compliance
Lightning Source LLC
Chambersburg PA
CBHW060540080526
44586CB00012B/800